Internet Security For Parents

Discover the Hidden Dangers That You and Your Children Face Online

Dan Ivancic

Internet Security For Parents

Copyright © 2008 by Dan Ivancic

Notice of Rights

Trademark Notice

Table of Contents

Introduction

Unfortunately, along with instant weather reports, stock updates, and breaking news, the information age also brings us weekly, if not daily reminders of sexual predators in our midst. In our frustration and disgust, we make comments about these predators on the news but may never actually do anything to stop or prevent them. Of course, there are exceptions like the FBI Cyber Crimes Task Force that works very hard to catch online predators and child pornography users.

There is also Dateline NBC that has been running the episode called "To Catch a Predator". On this popular TV show, they trick predators into thinking a real minor wants to have sexual relations with them but instead they end up exposed to millions of viewers on national TV and go to jail.

These efforts are great but the problem continues to escalate. I did a search for registered sex offenders in my area and there were almost 200 registered sex offenders. That's what compelled me to write this book. I want to help educate parents so they will know how to protect their kid's from online predators and the many other dangers online.

I believe that by educating parents and showing them how their kid's put themselves at risk without knowing it, I can help prevent kids from becoming victims.

Also it's not just your children that are at risk but parents face many risks online as well and your children may be to blame.

The outline of this book has been designed to help parents, teachers, and others quickly take the appropriate measures to protect children using online services.

Online Predators a Growing Problem

The Internet is an amazing tool when used properly but, like any tool, there is a right way and a wrong way to use it. There have been many recent advances in Internet technology including e-commerce, social networking, blogging, Web 2.0, instant messaging, video broadcasting, and undoubtedly there will be new technologies as trends and needs change

With well over 200 million people in North America alone using the Internet, the World Wide has become a virtual shopping mall for online predators. The following statistics should be enough to convince anyone that this is a real and growing threat to our children.

- One in five U.S. teenagers who regularly use the Internet say they have received unwanted sexual solicitations via the Web. Solicitations were defined as requests to engage in sexual activities or sexual talk, or to give personal sexual information.
  Crimes Against Children Research Center

- 25% of children have been exposed to unwanted pornographic material online.
  Crimes Against Children Research Center

- Only 1/3 of households with Internet access are actively protecting their children with filtering or blocking software.
  Center for Missing and Exploited Children

- 75% of children are willing to share personal information online about themselves and their family in exchange for goods and services.
  eMarketer

- Only approximately 25% of children who encountered a sexual approach or solicitation told a parent or adult.
  Crimes Against Children Research Center

- One in 33 youth received an aggressive sexual solicitation in the past year. This means a predator asked a young person to meet somewhere, called on the phone, and/or sent correspondence, money, or gifts through the U.S. Postal Service.
  Youth Internet Safety Survey

- 77% of the targets for online predators were age 14 or older. Another 22% were users ages 10 to 13.
  Crimes Against Children Research Center

The statistics show this is a real problem and it's only getting worse. Problems start when parents naively think "my kid would never talk to strangers online or worse yet meet someone in person that they've meet online". This kind of thinking puts our children at risk. Later in this book you'll see how predators have traced down kid's, kidnapped and raped them without ever communicating directly with the perpetrator. This is possible because children leave little clues out on the web that might seem harmless enough, but to someone with a dangerous mind like an online predator, the clues are all that is needed to trace down their victims.

Parents need to stop hiding in fear from computers and the Internet and start getting involved. This information is being made available to help parents protect their children. Parents can do their part by sharing this information with family; friends and teachers so that everyone can do their part to make our children's online experience a safer one.

Please keep in mind there is no profile for an online predator; they are people from all ages and walks of life. This may be the one thing that fools our vulnerable youth. Prevention is our best fighting chance to stop dangerous online predators.

Sex Offenders

Wouldn't you want to know if there was one living on your street?

There are tools available on the Internet to help locate sex offenders.

Your children should be warned and educated if these individuals are living near your home. After explaining the dangers that exist, pictures and addresses of individuals to be avoided should be shared.

Sex offenders monitor the activities and places frequented by children. Informing our youth about these individuals is our best defense, ignoring the problem will not make it go away.

There are many websites that offer the ability to search for registered sex offenders in your area. Most of these websites are free. Some will try to charge for this service but, there is no need to pay with useful free services available.

At the time this book was written, www.familywatchdog.us is a free service that provides the ability to do broad searches by zip code and even search your street. If you do not find that website helpful, visit google.com and try searching for (registered sex offender NY). Substitute your state abbreviation in the search and you should get your local governments registered sex offender website. Your local government website will have the most up to date list of any registered sex offenders or at least the ones that have been caught.

Preliminary Checks That Every Parent Needs to Do Online

The first step a parent should take is to see what kind of information about your child might be archived and stored on the major search engines. For anyone unfamiliar with what a search engine is. A search engine is an automated program that crawls the Internet for content, when content is found an index is created for that particular keyword. In simple terms, this is similar to an index in a library that allows one particular book to be found amidst thousands.

The three major search engines currently are Google (www.google.com), Yahoo (www.yahoo.com), and MSN (www.msn.com). Start with these 3 major search engines when searching for your child's information.

Start by typing your child's name in each one of these search engines. Click on each result that comes up for your search. As you click on each result, you should be looking for information that pertains to your child. If your child has a common name, it's possible you won't find much with this method but remember this is just a start.

If the 3 search engines do not return any information on your child, then your child may be cautious and smart with their online activity by not using their real or full name. Many online activities require the use of a screen name which is basically just as it sounds; it is made to screen out your real name so it gives you a little bit of anonymous security.

Try going back to the three main search engines and typing in a distinct nick name that your child may have for example (littlegreenjenny, littlegreenjenny91, littlegreenjenny1991, or littlegreenjenny16). That's generally what a typical screen name might look like try adding your child's date of birth or age into your guess for a screen name like I have done above.

Checking for Unfamiliar Software

One more preliminary search that you can do is to check for unfamiliar software that your child may have installed on your computer. Certain types of unfamiliar software may cause problems with your computer including tracking your personal information so that it can be used for identity theft purposes. The most common types of software children install on a computer is peer-to-peer software used for downloading music and software, as well as instant messaging software so they can chat with their friends online.

In Windows, you can click on the start button in the lower left-hand corner and then click on all programs and you should go through the list of programs and see if there are any unfamiliar programs that have been installed. Write down the names of the unfamiliar programs and do a search on the three major search engines to try and determine what they are used for, I'll cover more on this later in the book.

Your Childs Online Activity Aware of it or Not, They are Still Targets

Many children go online to hang out on social networking websites, create personal WebPages, start their own blog, communicate in online chat rooms, play games, listen to streaming music, and watch streaming videos. Although many of these activities may seem harmless, they can put your child in great risk online.

Many people, including both children and adults, create personal WebPages or blogs and visit online chat rooms for their topic of interest. Many people will share a lot of personal information on these pages about their interests, hobbies, likes and dislikes, as well as personal contact information. Usually the extent of personal information that people share is a screen name or an e-mail address. This usually is not a problem, but it can put you in danger if the wrong person gets a hold of it.

Many online predators and stalkers will try to warm up to a possible victim by pretending to have similar interests as that person. Many online predators are very manipulative and have convinced many young teenagers to meet them in person after they have first established a relationship online for a while. There are countless stories of young straight A honor roll students that have become victims because of this very same circumstance.

Young teens are especially vulnerable at this stage in their life. They are faced with stresses school, peer pressure, confrontation with other teens, drugs, sex, plans for college, trying to choose a career path, and sometimes family issues. Many teens turn to the internet to find someone that can understand them or just to find someone that shares similar interests or problems. Again this is usually harmless until a manipulative predator convinces them to take the next step. They become better friends by meeting face-to-face or sharing more personal information.

Parents must not be so naive to think that their child is smarter than this and that their child would never do such a thing. It's not always the child that agrees to meet their "New Friend", sometimes children just give out a little to much information and that's all it takes for a predator to find and abduct your child.

Every story and police report that I've heard and read the parent was always dumb founded that their Straight A child would do something so stupid. There's an old saying that says, "Trust but Verify" you can trust your child but you should verify that they are using the Internet in a safe and proper manor. Children don't always do the right thing and they will make mistakes. Hopefully by parents following the steps in this book they can help ensure that their child will not make any of these mistakes. I believe the best way to stop online predators is by educating parents and getting them involved.

Social Networking the Online Shopping Mall for Predators

Social networking consists of an interactive web application that will allow anybody to build their own network of friends where they can communicate and share their interests as well as any personal information they want to give. Social networking is a great way to keep in touch with friends, classmates, find long lost friends, and to find single people in your area.

A social networking website allows you to create your own profile where you post your photos, videos, information about your interests, write journals, and create a network of friends that allows everyone to communicate with each other.

Social networking is usually harmless if you are very cautious, but the problem is most young teens and young adults are not cautious when they use social networking websites and that is exactly what online predators are looking for.

There are several very popular social networking websites and you will see which the important ones are and what guidelines should be followed in order to help keep your children safe.

The first thing you need to do is familiarize yourself with the following websites (myspace.com, facebook.com, and friendster.com). These are some of the most widely used social networking websites. These may not be the only websites your children are using so later in this book I will tell you some methods to determine exactly which websites your children are using.

Myspace.com tends to be the most popular of the social networking websites especially with the younger audience. MySpace reported they have accumulated 67 million members since its launch in 2004, and their current growth rate is about 250,000 new members daily.

MySpace reported that roughly 80% of their users were 18 and older. That does not put these people at any less risk from a predator or stalker just because they are a little older. The age verification process on any social networking website relies on the honor system. Several MySpace profiles claim they are 99 years old or something ridiculous like that when they clearly belong to a young person. This would lead me to believe that MySpace's 80% figure is not accurate.

It is incredibly easy for anyone to signup for a new, free email account. It only takes a minute or two. If MySpace deletes the under age accounts they find, you can be assured the underage children will come back with a new email address to sign up for a new account.

MySpace has tried to maintain tight security policies, which users must adhere to; failure to adhere to their policies will result in termination of your MySpace account. MySpace requires its members to be at least 14 years or older to use their website but again many children get around this by lying about their age when they create their profile. MySpace now takes security measures by actively searching their user profiles for children under 14 that have created an account. Once they find under age users, their account is deleted. But this does not stop children from coming back to MySpace and signing up with a new email account and falsely reporting their age. The only real way to police these issues starts in the home with the parent's involvement.

MySpace reported they have 90 employees monitoring the safety and security of its members by using search algorithms to review profiles of members to try and pin point certain clues that help them find the underage children creating accounts. MySpace also limits the amount of information that can be displayed on a user's profile between the age of 14 and 16 years old. If you are between the age of 14 and 16, MySpace requires that your profile be set to private so that only friends in your network can view your profile. Individuals wanting access to your profile simply send a friend request to you which users have the capability to approve or deny a friend request.

Most kids enjoy having many friends in their network. If they approve all friend requests to gain these friends, it's no problem for a predator to gain access to your child's profile even if their profile is set to private.

Once someone is established as a friend in their network they can view all the information you have posted on your profile and communicate privately with that individual as well.

An online report told of a police detective who put the private registration on MySpace to the test by acting as a young peer and requesting to be a friend on several young teens MySpace profiles. The detective did this to prove that many young teens will freely accept anyone as a friend on his or her Myspace account. When the detective confronted the teens, they were shocked and frightened that the detective was able to track them down with the information they were sharing online. When the parents of the young teens were informed they were extremely frightened and embarrassed that this happened to their children. Each parent thought they had taken good security measures to keep their children safe online, but they were relieved that the detective brought this matter to their attention before an online predator did. The most important thing is prevention; you must take the necessary precautions to prevent any possible dangers for your children and yourself.

With 250,000 new members joining daily it's hard to imagine that 90 employees can effectively screen out most of the children under the age of 14. Their search algorithms are not going to pin point every under age child using their website. A quick test search found an entire network of 8 year old girls in which one of the girls was a somewhat famous model for TV commercials and magazine ads. She had her own MySpace account with a network of friends that were all her age, she also had her first and last name listed as well as the city and state where she lives and she posted a picture of her family's house.

With a little more online searching, predators can find addresses, phone numbers and other personal information

That's why parents enforcing ground rules on computers in their household is so important. It can mean life or death! The bottom line is that parents need to get involved and monitor their children's Internet activity and know what your child is doing online before someone else does.

Banning your children from MySpace and other social networking websites probably won't work either because where there's a will there's a way. Your child will find a way to use these websites with or without your permission. If you stop your child from using MySpace or other social networking websites, it may prompt your child to setup another profile online and start using social networking websites without your knowledge on a different computer that you can't monitor like at a friend's house. If you can't see what they are doing online then it's going to be like driving a car blindfolded; you're going to lose control.

You might be better off allowing your children to use MySpace with your permission and with your guidelines and rules which you are learning from this book. That way you can monitor what they are doing easier and you'll always be in control of what's going on. I've heard of parents deleting their child's MySpace profile or changing their password so their child can no longer access it. Again, I generally don't recommend this because your child most likely will create another account and be a little more cautious this time so you can't find his or her account.

Once this happens you pretty much lose control of the situation. You might be thinking the whole time that you solved the problem when you really just made it worse because now you are no longer monitoring your child's social networking and Internet activities. It is always better to work with your child to mutually create a safe online experience. There is a time however when you may need to step in and delete or lock your child out of their MySpace account. Specifically, this is anytime you feel that your child is at serious danger or has been chatting with an online predator. If you ever see substantial evidence that your child has been chatting with an online predator please contact your local police authorities. One important thing to look for is if anyone online has asked your child to meet them in person. This will be discussed along with several more warning signs that should help you determine if your child is at risk in Chapter 5.

Another feature of social networking websites that should be of great concern to parents is private communication. This has been made possible via built in email, instant messaging, and chat rooms in MySpace and other websites. These three utilities will make it hard for you to see if your child has been communicating with a potential online predator. Usually you need your child's login information, which is the email address they have registered and their password. Without their log in information you will not be able to see who they have been talking to. The good news is there is a solution that is covered in full detail in Chapter 6.

Just a quick note, MySpace is mentioned frequently because it's the most popular social networking website that kid's use. Most of the guidelines and rules recommended can be applied to any social networking website.

Some Guidelines and Rules That Should Be Followed for Using Social Networking Websites

1.) Never use your full name where it may be visible to the public.

Your child should never list their full name on their MySpace profile, doing so makes it easy for a predator or stalker to search the white pages online and find your home address.

2.) Never identify the school that you attend.

Many social networking websites allow you to identify the school that you attend; this is usually not considered a big deal but consider this possible dangerous scenario. If your child plays a school sport then a predator would know what school your child attends, and most school sporting events are public knowledge. Any predator or stalker will instantly know your child's schedule and because they've seen your child's profile online they know exactly what your child looks like. All it would take is a late night school sports game or for your child to be caught walking alone for just one minute. Identifying your school is a feature most useful to people who have been out of high school for a while and are trying to get in touch with old friends. If your child is currently attending school there is no reason to list what school they attend because all their friends already know that.

3.)   Never identify where you work.

Most social networking websites also allow you to list where you work. This is yet again another way for a predator or stalker to pin point your child. I was listening to an FBI Agent from the Cyber Crimes Task Force give a presentation on this mater and she said she dealt with a case where a young female girl had posted where she worked on her MySpace profile. A predator used that info to stalk the female victim late at night when she got out of work and most unfortunately while walking to her car the online predator raped her.

4.)   Never display your email or instant messaging screen name.

Unsuspecting children routinely list their email or instant messaging screen name asking people to contact them if their interested in chatting. Predators use children's profiles on their social networking accounts to contact them via email or instant messaging. Remember a profile is what social networking websites use to let your child describe their likes, interests, hobbies, and any other information they want to list. Once a predator knows this they will contact your child and try to become a friend by pre-tending to have similar interests as your child. Online predators may start off with a soft approach by acting as if they are new to the area and looking to make some friends or just find out about some fun things to do in the area.

5.)   Know your child's online addresses and screen names

You should know your child's email address as well as any screen names they might use for instant messaging. You should also know what your child's MySpace Name or MySpace address is, MySpace will let you create a name that essentially gives you your own space on myspace.com, this allows your profile to be accessible from a web address e.g. (www.myspace.com/whateveryouwant). If your child is not stubborn and will willingly give you this information it will make it easier for you to supervise and make sure your child is not making any mistakes. If your child tries to be stubborn and tells you that's private information and they don't want you snooping through their stuff, don't panic you'll see possible solutions to this problem later in this book.

6.)   Know who's in your child's friends list

Look at your child's MySpace profile and navigate to the section that has all of their friends listed. Click on each one and see if there are any questionable looking friends listed on your child's profile. Look for the obvious things first which would include looking to see if any of your child's friends are in a different city or state, also look for anyone that might be noticeably older than your child.

Online predators will undoubtedly create a false profile with an alluring youthful picture so the age check won't always work. If you can be open with your child about the process of reviewing their friends, sit down with them and have them explain who each of their friends are and how they know them as well as how they met them. If you look at the number of friends that are listed on your child's profile and the number is in the hundreds that should draw a red flag. Try comparing the number of friends listed on their profile to the number of students in their grade level. From my own high school experience, schools have several cliques and chances are that your child has blended into one of them. If you are unfamiliar with cliques, they are basically a small exclusive group of friends that stick together. One example is the jocks or guys and girls that play sports will typically be good friends with a few exceptions. Similarly your child's friend list on their profile should parallel their social life, a small tight group of friends would be normal.

Before closing the chapter on social networking websites, I'd like to share a local news story from my hometown Buffalo NY that illustrates just how dangerous these websites can be. The story came to light while writing this book.

A 48-year-old cafeteria worker created his own MySpace page and disguised himself as a muscular 20-year-old male. He called himself "sex master Adam". The picture that he posted on his profile was of course not his real picture but a picture of a young muscular 20-year-old male with his shirt off.

His personal profile read "Yes I am from Buffalo. What I'm looking for are some bad girls and when I say bad I mean really bad girls who will do anything I ask them to."

The police reported that there were dozens of responses from teenage girls, some of them as young as 13. The sexual predator was able to convince these young girls to send nude pictures of themselves in obscene poses; he was also able to get some of the girl's cell phone numbers. Most of the girls would start out sending topless pictures of themselves. When he asked for more and they refused he threatened to tell their parents and post all of their information and pictures they sent him for the rest of the world to see. If they wouldn't show him what he wanted, he even threatened some of the girls that he would come to their house and kill them if they would not send more nude photos.

Police believe after looking at all of the photos the sexual predator received on his cell phones and computer that there might have been more than 100 girls who willingly subjected themselves to the manipulative sexual predator.

Can you imagine more than 100 girls, some as young as 13 in one city sending totally nude photos to strangers they don't know online? Why are kids looking for love in all the wrong places?

One reason why this is possible is that many parents don't monitor their children's Internet activity. Some may not know where to start if they wanted to. Again, my motivation for writing this book is to educate parents and bring to light the many dangers that family's faces in the Internet world.

The main reason for sharing this alarming story was to alert parents of the real importance of knowing your child's Internet activities.

In the digital age we now live in, many children have their own digital cameras and webcams which make it very easy to share pictures and videos publicly online or send them privately to other people.

If you want to know everything your child is doing online without alarming your child, take a look at the software made available on my website. This software will give you the ability to see every email, instant message, chat room, web site, usernames, passwords, and etc... that your child types in the computer without your child knowing that you are monitoring their activity.

www.InternetSecurityForParents.com/software

An Action Plan if You Think Your Child Might be at Risk

First things first, it is important to know some basic warning signs that indicate your child is at risk to online predators.

Your child is receiving unusual or expensive gifts.

If an online predator has an interest in your child they may try to attract child with expensive gifts. The gifts may be sent through the mail since they have not meet in person the intention of a predator is to gain trust and establish a "friendship". If you discover your child is receiving gifts from a stranger, an online relationship has already been established. Contact your local police authorities and the FBI immediately. If the police or the FBI agrees this is an online predator they may need your assistance uncovering as much information as possible to arrest the predator. By turning this information over to the authorities not only would you be protecting your child but you may be protecting the lives of countless other children.

Someone online posing as a new "friend" has approached your child.

Online predators will try to make "friends" with your child to gain their trust and obtain their ultimate goal, which is to con your child into meeting in person. If you are monitoring your child's Internet activity using the steps described in Chapter 6 you will know if and when this happens.

Your child fears someone may be stalking them.

Predators use the information trails that children leave online to track them down and force their will on them. Use the information in the previous chapters to make sure your child is not posting any information that a predator could use to find them. If either you or your child is worried that someone may be stalking him/her, then you should contact your local police immediately.

Your child is very secretive or private about their Internet use and activities.

If your child is hiding or being very private about their Internet activities, then there's probably something that you should know about. Kids use instant messaging and abbreviated phrases when talking to their friends, along with faster typing; it makes it hard for parents to understand what they're talking about. Instant messaging will be covered in greater detail in Chapter 11.

What You Can Do if Your Child is Stubborn

It's always best to review your concerns about online dangers with your child, but undoubtedly there will be plenty of kid's who will not be open to this kind of discussion with their parents.

Some kid's feel they have the right to keep their Internet activities private from their parents. For your child's safety, step in and take control. This can be done without your child knowing. Your child doesn't make the rules in the house and they shouldn't make the rules on the computer either.

First, try checking your child's internet history and temporary internet files, this should show you each website your child has visited recently. You can check your computers Internet history very easily if you use Internet Explorer. If your computer does not use Internet Explorer you should have a comparable Internet browser that will allow you to view your Internet history, check your help documentation on your Internet browser if you are having difficulty locating your Internet history.

1. Click the black drop down arrow to the right of the Back and Forward button.
2. Click the History tab at the bottom of the menu.

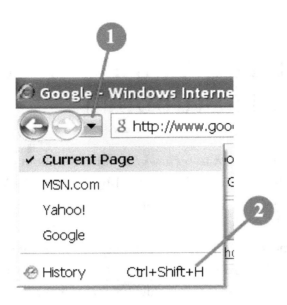

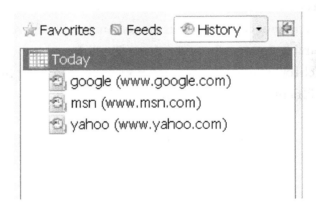

Once you click on History on the left column it will give you some date range options so you can see which websites were visited and when they were visited as shown in the next picture.

One important point, the Internet History is not fool proof because many kid's know how to delete their Internet history, you can see for yourself how easy it is to delete if you right click on any website listed in the History it will give you an option to delete it.

If you click on all the date ranges in the History tab and websites are not displayed this too should raise a warning flag. Your child could be trying to cover their tracks before you're able to check it. By default Internet Explorer usually keeps 20 days of Internet History on file.

If you didn't find any Internet History recorded you may want to check the Temporary Internet Files, again this is not fool proof and your child might be deleting these as well, but you can still check.

How to check your Temporary Internet Files

1.   Open Internet Explorer

**Internet
Explorer**

2.   Click on Tools

3.   Click Internet Options

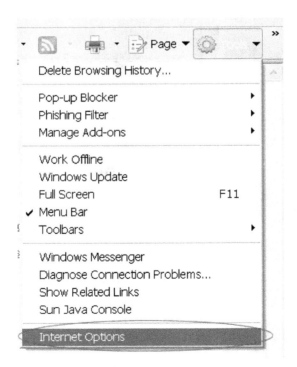

4. Under Browsing History click on Settings

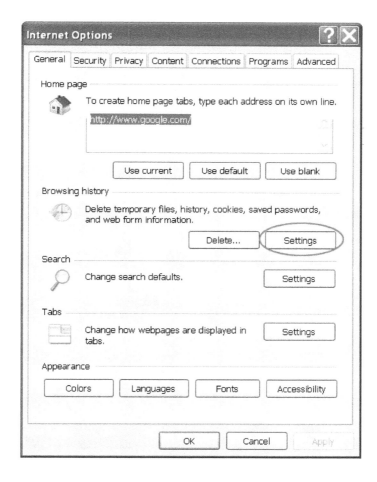

5. Click View Files

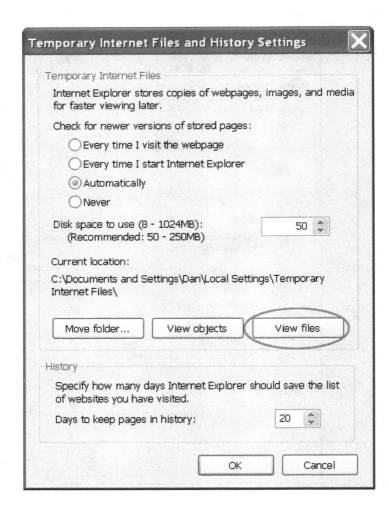

With the file display box open, look at the Internet address for each of the files. This will basically show you which websites have been visited for that user on the computer.

One solution for parents with stubborn children is to use computer monitoring software, which I have made available for the readers of this book through my website at www.InternetSecurityForParents.com/software.

This software will give you the ability to monitor all activity on your computer, capture all keystrokes, programs used, websites visited and take screenshots of all computer use.

The software runs completely invisible and is easy to use. All information captured is stored in an encrypted log file, which can be sent secretly at scheduled intervals to any specified email address.

All activity in Internet Explorer can be monitored, and Web pages are stored for viewing offline.

Here are a couple more features that make this software the best possible solution for monitoring a stubborn child's Internet activity or if you suspect there might be a problem.

- Screenshots can be taken at given intervals, capturing everything that is currently on the screen.
- Monitor your computer while you are away, retrieve lost information; monitor your children's activity, and much more!

Features:
- NEW: Now compatible with GMail!
- Capture keystrokes
- Capture programs used
- Capture websites in Internet Explorer
- Capture screenshots

- Encrypted log file – your child won't be able to delete them
- Secretly email log files
- Invisible Stealth Mode – your child won't know its running
- Unique playback mode lets you view captured keystrokes, programs, WebPages, screenshots in real time
- Run silently at startup
- Auto-capture at startup

In addition to reading this book and educating yourself, consider investing in protecting your child and yourself from the many online dangers by purchasing this software at:

www.InternetSecurityForParents.com/software

Online Actions That Can Permanently Affect Your Childs Future Career

As discussed earlier in this book, many children use social networking websites like MySpace.com. Although these websites attract many children, the information posted on them is not always proper and might affect your child's future career possibilities.

Some children go through phases in their life where they follow trends that make them change their personal image, i.e. the gothic look where kids dress in all black, get all kinds of piercings and etc... or maybe they go for the baggy clothes rapper look. These trends tend to be displayed in not only their own personal image but in places like their bedroom where you might see their bedroom take on a similar look. This is all fairly standard and nothing out of the ordinary. The other place that kids tend to display their self-interests is online through the use of social networking websites or blogs, which are becoming increasingly popular. The problem that this can create is that the Internet basically becomes an archive; anything that gets published on the Internet has a great chance of being found years later. Basically to sum this up, there are countless MySpace profiles where kid's post pictures of marijuana leaves and all kinds of other obscene and inappropriate content.

One problem with this is when your child goes to apply for a job after college many human resource departments now check social networking websites and archives on the Internet to find out a little bit more about their potential job candidate. If they find the obscene content from your child's past, they won't get that job. I know this for a fact because I have assisted companies in finding this information. In fact, I recently have seen a case where a company had two potential job candidates and when a MySpace profile for one of the potential candidates had pictures of several different popular brands of alcohol the candidate was ruled out. In general, when a profile shows any candidate to be questionable you can guess who will get the job. The important thing to remember is that your child should never post anything online that a future employer might frown upon.

Web 2.0 and why it can be Harmful to Your Child

Web 2.0 is composed of increasingly popular web-based communities that are changing the Internet as we know it today. These web-based communities are typically geared and reliant upon participation of younger users that share their information, input, and creativity with other users. Because most Web 2.0 sites typically appeal to a younger audience, this can be another resource that online predators may use to prey on unsuspecting children.

There are several very popular web 2.0 platforms that are used, social networking which was already discussed earlier in this book, blogs, and other copycat social networking websites similar to MySpace. There are other web 2.0 platforms like social book marking and wikis but currently these haven't shown any real dangers. The focus of this book is to point out any possible dangers that you or your children might face online.

The Internet is constantly changing and new advances are being made all of the time. I plan on keeping purchasers of this book updated about any new advances being made as well as any new serious potential threats you and your kids may face. Details on how to get free updates will be listed at the end of this book.

For now we'll focus on blogs, why they are so popular, and the potential dangers they can bring.

A blog is a web log or a web journal that someone writes in chronological order, and they have become increasingly popular because they are extremely easy to use, and don't require any programming to setup most of them. Many "Bloggers" just like to rant and rave and hear themselves talk while others read what they're blogging about.

Many individuals will use a blog like a journal and typically write about their likes, dislikes, and personal life. With a blog, a person can talk about whatever they want. There are no limitations and that's what can make a blog potentially dangerous. If your child starts his or her own blog, they should be careful not to share too much of their personal information like where they attend school, where they work, or what school sports they play. Sharing personal information makes it much easier to track someone down in person.

Again remember with blogs there usually is no one monitoring them, unlike the social networking websites like MySpace where there are at least some guidelines that children have to follow. Blogs are basically a free-for-all. If your child has setup a blog, you should definitely monitor that as well.

The most popular blogs are the hosted service blogs because they don't require users any programming to set these up and you don't need your own domain name. If your child was going to setup their own blog, they would probably use one of the following: www.blogger.com, www.livejournal.com, or www.wordpress.com. These are some of the most popular blog services.

If you want to find a personal blog that your child has started you can try www.technorati.com which is basically a search engine for blogs. A recent search showed that they have tracked more than 105 million blogs. Try typing your child's name or nicknames into the search bar at the top of www.technorati.com. If your child has a blog and it has any presence, then there is a good chance that you will find it here, assuming of course that your child has posted his or her name on their blog.

Another resource to check is the three major search engines google.com, yahoo.com, and msn.com. Start by typing your child's name in each one of these search engines and click on each result that comes up for your search, as you click on each one you should be looking for information that pertains to your child. If your child has a common name like "John Smith", it's possible that you won't find much that is related to your child.

AOL People Connection

AOL People Connection (http://peopleconnection.aol.com/main/) is basically another social networking site similar to MySpace and they definitely are not the only ones jumping on the social networking band-wagon. Their website offers many of the same features that MySpace does including of course the social networking, photo posting, blogs, and message boards. If you want to search for your child on their website, click on the link above, then click on the "Profiles" tab, finally type your child's name, city, and state you live in. There usually will be several pages of results so make sure you look through all of them.

If you do not see any results listed, that doesn't mean your child has not created a profile on AOL People Connection. It may indicate your child has not listed their full name, and may be using a screen name or their profile name instead (which is a good practice).

If you would like to eliminate all of the guess work, then I highly recommend that you visit my website www.InternetSecurityForParents.com/software and take a look at the computer monitoring software that I have listed. The software has the ability tell you which websites your child visits, what passwords they type in, the email messages they send, what they type in chat rooms, and basically everything that happens on the computer. The best feature is that the software runs discretely every time the computer is started and your child will never know its running. If feel it's wrong to be secretly recording all of your child's Internet activity, it's always better to be safe than sorry. The only time you may find it necessary to inform them is if you notice any of the dangerous indicators I have discussed in this book. Remember what you don't know can hurt you and your child; sometimes tough love is the best love you can give your child.

Kid's Internet Activities that are Costing Parents $5,000+ in Lawsuits

Many kids are under the mistaken impression that protected music and movies that have to be purchased in stores are available for free on the Internet. However, there are potentially serious problems attached to downloading unauthorized copies of music and movie files from the Internet. Anyone downloading these illegally shared files is risking damaging lawsuits by doing so.

The number of parents and children that have found themselves facing lawsuits due to these activities is growing. The music industry stopped disclosing national figures but as of spring in 2006 there were more than 18,000 people that had lawsuits filed against them and the record companies are not stopping there efforts on stopping and punishing those who partake in illegal file sharing. The Internet has made it very easy to illegally share files through the use of P2P (peer to peer) software. Millions of illegally shared files are being downloaded and it takes just a few minutes. This is why P2P services are growing in popularity even though most users know it's illegal.

The RIAA (Recording Industry Association of America) and the Motion Picture Association of America has been fighting back strong against those downloading music and movies illegally and they don't care if it's a young person doing it or an adult.

Peer-to-Peer file sharing basically works by having thousands of users sharing their files through P2P software they have installed voluntarily. The problem is that these P2P networks are open to the public, so the RIAA got smart and is now actively monitoring these file sharing activities. Once they find people sharing unauthorized music files, they will subpoena your Internet Service Provider who then, according to the DMCA (The Digital Millennium Copyright Act), must supply the name and address of the person registered on the Internet account in violation. In many cases this is the parent of the household. Once this happens, you're pretty much up the creek with out a paddle and you may be sued for thousands of dollars. The lawsuit depends on the severity of the case, but the majority of the violators or their parent's typically end up settling for $5,000 + legal fees. Parents are usually held responsible for their kid's Internet activities. If you've never read the terms of service or AUP (Acceptable Use Policy) from your Internet Service Provider, then you should do so ASAP.

If your child has an iPod or any other mp3 player that is loaded with music and you have no idea how they're getting this music, then you better ask. In some cases, your child may copy the music from a CD they already own which is fine. If your child tells you they get all of their music online and you know it wasn't paid for, then you better take immediate action and remove any P2P programs from any computer in your household.

Every parent should be able to identify P2P programs installed on their computer. We'll discuss the most popular P2P programs and learn a quick way to find them on a computer with a Windows operating system.

The most popular P2P programs are eDonkey / Overnet, Shareaza, WinMX, BitTorrent, Limewire, Morpheus, eMule, Ares, BearShare, Kazaa, iMesh, Red Swoosh, and Groove.

The P2P programs listed above are not the only ones and you can be assured there will be new P2P programs developed so you should start looking to see if any of these major programs are installed on your computer or your child's computer. You should know what every program on your computer is and what it's used for. If there are programs installed on your computer and you are uncertain about their use try searching for the name of the program using a search engine and you should be able to find some information on what the program is used for.

To review all of the programs installed on your computer follow the steps listed below:

1.)   Click the windows start button

2.) Click on All Programs and you should see a list of all the programs installed on your computer.

Programs blurred for security reasons

2.)   Review all of the programs listed, checking for the most common P2P programs we discussed in the beginning of this chapter.

If you find a P2P program installed on your computer, you should talk to your child about what they use it for and why they installed it. Any P2P programs should be removed immediately. Downloading illegally shared files is not worth the risk of damaging lawsuits and it is breaking the law! Another point of great concern is these files are often not what they claim to be. A common practice used by hackers is to embed these files with privacy-invasive software (spyware), viruses, and other threats that may steal your personal information, compromise your security, and/or damage your computer and any data stored on it.

Unsecured Wireless Internet

Wireless Internet devices provide the ability to access the Internet on your computer without having to run wires through your walls. Laptop users with wireless features enabled can take their computer just about anywhere in the house and still access the Internet.

Many home computer users not familiar with wireless Internet features will typically take the wireless router or similar device out of the box, simply plug it in, and start using it without setting up any security measures. One pitfall with the wireless Internet is that when it's not secured properly anyone in your neighborhood or anybody passing by in a car can use your Internet connection to do whatever they want.

Recent searches have turned up people being sued by the RIAA for thousands of dollars for sharing and downloading unauthorized music files. The puzzling thing to these individuals was they never even heard of P2P software, they had no idea what it was used for and it was not installed on their computer. They also had no clue about downloading music.

You may ask "How did they end up getting sued for something they didn't do?" The answer is someone in their neighborhood or someone in a car near their house with a laptop connected to their unsecured wireless Internet and started downloading and sharing illegal music files.

These individuals were actually innocent but still had to fight the lawsuit in court and hope they could prove their case. Fighting these lawsuits may end up costing you more money then the typical $5,000 - $10,000 settlement that the record companies are usually looking to settle for. One woman has paid out over $24,000 in legal fees fighting a lawsuit and has not won her case yet.

To determine if your wireless Internet connection is secured you should follow the steps below:

1.)   Click the Windows start button

2.)   Click the Control Panel button

3.)   Double click the Network Connections button

Network
Connections

4.)   Make sure your Wireless Network Connection shows the secure lock in the upper right corner

Wireless Network
Connection

If you are still uncertain, consult the owner's manual for your wireless router. Each router's security setup is different and it is beyond the scope of this book to list them all. Entire books have been dedicated to wireless Internet security.

Even if you are connecting your computer to the Internet by a wired connection like Ethernet or USB, you should still check to see if you have wireless features enabled. Most modems supplied by ISP's now feature wireless Internet capability. Consult your ISP or instruction manual if you are uncertain.

You may feel the need to hire a professional computer consultant to configure your computer security and setup needs. After finishing this book, you'll have a better idea about which recommendations to have a professional help you with.

If you want to take on computer administration tasks yourself, you may want to consult other materials that specialize on your topics of interest. The "For Dummies" series of books is well written and easy to understand. If, for example, your operating system is Windows XP, you may want to pick up "Windows XP for Dummies". If you are interested in wireless Internet security you may find the book "Wireless Home Networking for Dummies" useful.

Remember, as stated in the "Terms of Service" of most ISP's, you are responsible for your Internet connection and how it's used! Make sure everyone in your household is using it properly and verify that your computers security is setup and configured properly or have a professional help with the settings.

Identity Theft Problems for Parents – Are Your Kid's to Blame?

Many kids dominate the home computer today. Not only can this lead to certain dangers for your kid's, as discussed in previous chapters, but it can also lead to serious identity theft problems for parents.

Identity theft is one of the fastest growing crimes in the world and it has devastating financial effects on its victims. Victims of identity theft typically do not discover they've become a victim until 14 months after their identity has been stolen. In that 14-month period, their credit history will most likely be destroyed and replaced with massive unpaid debts. Many victims of identity theft spend several months or even several years trying to reestablish their credit score. Until the victims credit score has been restored, they will find it incredibly difficult to obtain an apartment, secure any kind of loan, obtain a checking account, and in some instances victims find it difficult to find employment.

When you become a victim of identity theft your whole life on paper is destroyed and many victims spend thousands of dollars in legal fees trying to reestablish themselves.

So why is identity theft such a fast growing problem? It may be because our security measures are struggling to keep pace with the advances in computer technology. A large number of computer users are not informed about the many dangers on the Internet and these users are the main targets for identity thieves and computer hackers.

Your personal information may be stored in any number of computers and databases from electronic activities like online banking, bill payment, shopping, and many other daily tasks we use the computer for. Computers and the Internet have made our business and personal lives more efficient, much easier, and will continue to do so as technology continues to advance.

Unfortunately, the increase in online transactions also brings an increase in computer fraud and identity theft. In talking with many adults it's alarming to see how little thought is given to identity theft and computer security.

Let's discuss some measures to help prevent this from happening to you.

Spyware (Also known as Adware, Malware, Badware, Worms, Trojan Horses, and Computer Virus)

You can probably tell by the name "Spyware" exactly what this software does. Spyware is software that is installed on your computer covertly without your permission and sometimes installed sneakily with your permission. The software's usual purpose is to spy and record as much information as possible such as, banking information, credit card numbers, your social security number, and etc...

Spyware can also take complete control of your computer and compromise its operating system which can cause any number of the following problems:

- Slow Internet connection speeds
- Disallow other essential software to be installed and updated
- Install other spyware programs
- Change your home page on your web browser
- Redirect you to websites you did not request
- Cause many ads to pop up on your computer
- Erase critical data and programs
- Steal personal information and forward it to any number of people by email, or Internet communications

You might ask "How does spyware get installed on your computer?" The answer may very well be **Your Children**.

Many kids download free programs, free games and if your children are downloading free music and movies, as discussed in Chapter 9, then you can be fairly certain spyware has been loaded on your computer. To compound the problem most spyware programs play many dangerous roles on your computer.

Take for instance kid's who use P2P software to download music, not only do they put themselves and their parents at serious legal risk, but they also install various spyware programs which put their parents at risk to identity theft.

The saying "you get what you pay for" holds true here. Things you download for free are not always really free; sometimes there are hidden costs that you'll pay like infecting your computer with spyware.

Kids should not have permission to install programs on the computer without an adult's approval and we'll talk about that in Chapter 12 and how you can go about enforcing this automatically.

The next issue covered in this chapter is not typically targeted at younger children; instead this danger preys on unsuspecting adult Internet users and is a major cause of identity theft.

Phishing Email Scams

Phishing scams are targeted through email and prey on unsuspecting Internet users. The scammers send out emails that mirror a well known website like eBay, Bank of America, or PayPal just to name a few. The email will inform you that you need to update your account information and will provide a link for you to click on to update your account information. When unsuspecting Internet users click the link they're tricked into entering personal information because the website has a familiar look.

What happens next is the scam artist hijacks the account you just supplied the information for which allows them to have their way with your account and totally take control of it. If it was your bank account they are going to empty it, if it was your eBay account they will have fun shopping under your name, and etc...

Please note that any important online account like your banking, eBay, PayPal, or any other online account that stores your personal information will never send you an email asking you to update your account information. If they needed you to update or change your account information they would typically prompt you to do so the next time you logged in. To be on the safe side you may want to read the security policies that are provided for your important online accounts, every major company makes this information accessible on their website.

How to identify a phishing email

Take a look at the picture below carefully and I'll explain what you need to be looking for.

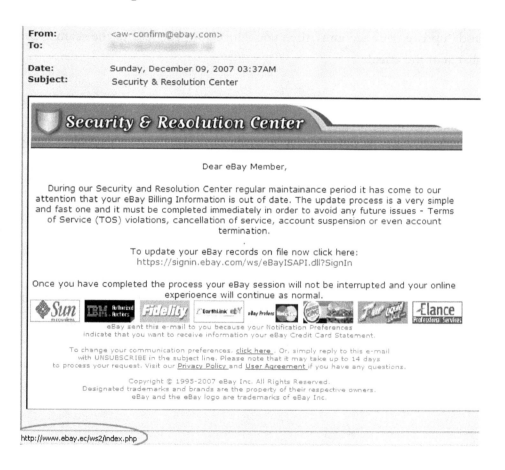

If you take a look at the [From:] field in the email it claims the email came from eBay.com and I assure you it did not. Also if you look at the body of the email you will notice the phishing scammer made it look like an official email you might receive from eBay.

Read the paragraph and you will see how these phishing scammers are very manipulative and scare you by saying if you don't update your information you will lose your account. The truth is if you do click that link and "update your account" then you'll lose your account to the scam artist that sent the email.

If you receive a suspicious email like this another suggestion is hover your mouse courser over the link and look at the status bar in the lower left hand corner that is circled in red. You should notice a website address and if you look at the domain name you will notice it does not say ebay.com but instead it says ebay.ec and this is one of the easiest and quickest ways to identify a phishing email.

The latest spyware scam

In this scam cyber criminals leverage YouTube's familiarity to their benefit and infect computers with their latest version of the Storm Worm computer virus. Basically the cyber criminal's blast out thousands of emails and in the subject line the email claims to be a cool new video on YouTube. By leveraging the YouTube name they've already warmed you up to clicking on the link in the email.

Many users who end up clicking the link are expecting to be watching a funny video on YouTube, but to their surprise they soon find that their computer has just been infected with a nasty computer virus.

This virus takes over complete control of your computer and starts attacking other computers on the Internet, the virus may also spam out spyware and junk email, attack other innocent computers, or run as spyware on your machine and steal all of your personal information. Cyber criminals use these viruses to make millions of dollars, which are stolen from unsuspecting Internet users like you.

This latest scam is just proof that cyber criminals are always creating manipulative ways to infect our computers with viruses.

To be informed of new dangers and threats that are constantly arising please visit our website below for FREE BOOK UPDATES. www.InternetSecurityForParents.com/freeupdates

When you sign up for our Free Updates, we will notify you as soon as we learn of new dangers or online threats. We are committed to keeping you informed and updated for FREE, available only to people who have purchased this book.

Instant Messaging and Chat Room Dangers

There are so many different methods used for online communications that it is beyond the scope of this book to cover them all. The most popular methods will be discussed in this chapter along with the dangers that can be faced with each one.

First, let's start by talking about some ground rules that you and your children should follow for any type of online communication.

Never list your full real name, address, telephone number, or any other personal information.

Many of the different forms of online communication can be archived and viewed by other people with the exception of email, which is usually a private form of online communication. The important thing to remember is if you don't want your personal information available to the public, don't type it or post it online. After posting your personal information online it would be very easy for anyone to use a search engine and find everything that you've posted.

Never agree to meet anyone in person that you've met online.

Online users start chatting online to meet people that share similar interests. In many cases they eventually end up developing a trusting friendship with the people they chat with online. Online predators and stalkers try to establish "friendships" with all types of unsuspecting people and their victims are off varied ages so parents and children beware.

Never accept files from people you don't know online, be very weary accepting files even from people you do know.

People often use instant messaging and other online chat programs to share files, whether its music files, movies, or software. The most common files shared are usually shared illegally meaning that they are files that you should be paying for. The risk involved is that not everyone is sharing files that you or your children might be looking for. For example, if your child is looking to download their favorite movie online and they find someone that claims to have it, they might send this person an instant message requesting the movie file. Next thing that can happen is when the movie file is sent to your child and they open it expecting their favorite movie instead a computer virus is installed that compromises your computer.

If this happens, your child probably won't inform you. Instead they'll pretend like nothing happened and the next time you check your online banking or purchase something online, your identity may be stolen.

People are not always who they say they are.

An online source reported the case of a woman who met a man online, they started dating, and neither of them had played the online dating game before. The woman was telling all of her friends what a great guy he was, a good-looking man, he had a good job at a bank, and he loved kids. One of her friends suggested she do a background check to see if he was as good as he seemed. The background check revealed that he was a registered sex offender; he did have a job at a big bank as a janitor, and about the only thing that held true was that you might say he was an attractive looking man. Looks can be deceiving. Make sure you and your children are aware that the people you chat with online are not always who they say they are.

Don't post information online that you wouldn't want your friends, family, online predators, employer, or future employer to find out.

Both kids and young adults at times like to post things they do online. For example a myspace.com site search for "4:20", pronounced four-twenty (the term stands for the consumption of marijuana) produced a video some young kid's posted of themselves smoking marijuana. Imagine a potential employer finding this kind of activity while investigating a potential candidate online.

Use aliases or screen names when chatting online.

When chatting or posting information online through the various chat methods you will usually be required to create a unique profile for yourself. Never use your real name when chatting or posting information online, instead create a screen name like jls12345. When you create an anonymous screen name it's much harder to be personally identified than if you used your full name or even part of your name.

Different chat methods used today

The most widely used methods of online communication used today are Email, Instant Messaging, ICQ, Chat Rooms, Forums and Discussion Groups. Let's take a look at each of the popular methods that your kid's are probably using and what impact they can have on your child.

Email

Email is by far the most popular form of online communication today and I hope by now you are familiar with it. If you are not yet familiar with email then you should think about picking up a book about it. There are many solutions available for sending and receiving email but the most popular ones use desktop software like Microsoft Outlook, Outlook Express, or many of the free web based email systems like Yahoo, Hotmail, and Gmail.

In case you're not familiar with this popular form of online communication, email stands for electronic mail and basically it gives you the ability to send messages, pictures, and files to anybody else with an email address.

Email can be very dangerous when your child is sharing his/her email address on public resources like social networking websites, blogs, and chat rooms just to name a few. The danger is that if an online predator takes interest in your child and gets his/her email address, a path of communication is opened that the online predator will use to start deceiving and manipulating your child until a bond of "friendship" is formed with your child.

Remember the statistics listed in Chapter One? Don't let your child be one of them! You should know your child's email address and monitor your child's email account, even if you have to do it discreetly as discussed in Chapter 6.

Instant Messaging

Instant messaging or IM for short makes instant communications possible with other users that are currently online. With instant messaging popularized by many young teens and adults, users can see who is online and chat in real time.

Many instant messaging systems allow for a web-cam setup allowing those you are chatting with to see you live over the Internet. If your child has a web-cam, make sure you know why they need it and how they are using it.

The most popular instant messaging services are AOL Instant Messenger also know as AIM, Windows Live Messenger, Skype, ICQ, Paltalk, Yahoo Messenger, and MySpaceIM. There are many other instant messaging services and I highly recommend you check your computer to see if any of these popular services are being used.

Another important fact to be aware of is that web-based email services commonly offer instant messaging right through your online account and it's not always necessary to install software on your computer to instant message other users. You should always monitor your child's computer activity using the steps discussed throughout this book. If you want to be absolutely certain about who your child is talking with online then you should use the monitoring software listed on our website.

www.InternetSecurityForParents.com/software

To make things even more complicated, many cell phone service providers have integrated popular instant messaging platforms like AIM into their cell phone plans. If your children have cell phones they may be able to use instant messaging unmonitored through their cell phone. If you are paying the bill, then you should contact your cell phone provider to see if instant messaging is available and if it can be monitored.

Another note on the popularity of instant messaging, AOL Instant Messenger has reported over 100 million registered users and 53 million active users, the other popular services have also reported high numbers of registered users like AIM.

This does not necessarily indicate that your child should not use instant messaging, but they should never post their instant messaging screen names on public places online like their MySpace profile page. Your child should also be aware that people they're chatting with are not always who they say they are. Also, they must never agree to meet anyone in person that they've met online and never give out any personal information online.

Another possible danger that parents face if their child uses instant messaging improperly is identity theft. Children frequently use instant messaging for file sharing and they will seek people online with the latest movie, or particular music tracks they may be looking for. The problem starts when your child finds a stranger online who "has what they were looking for". Files received from strangers online may infect your computer with spyware which in many cases runs silently in the background recording all of your personal information.

Chat Rooms

Chat rooms are similar to instant messaging but, instead of one-to-one messaging, chat rooms are typically intended for an entire group of people who would like to chat publicly. Everyone reads what people in chat rooms are typing in real time.

Chat rooms usually cater to a topic of interest like "Dating" or just about any other topic you could imagine. Certain topics may draw children to the chat room, which makes this resource yet another tool that pedophiles and online predators use to lure children into meeting them in person.

There are far too many chat rooms to list in this book because virtually anyone can setup a chat room on their website. You can find some of the most popular ones by going to Google.com and searching for "chat" or "chat room".

Many children use acronyms or chat abbreviations when they're instant messaging or chatting with someone online. This not only makes communication faster but it conceals their conversations from parents unaware of the meaning of theses acronyms. For example, a child may type "PAW" (parents are watching) or "P911" (parents in the room) which warns the person they are chatting with to keep the conversation and any pictures they are sharing appropriate.

If you would like a list of abbreviations that many children use, the National Center for Missing & Exploited Children has published a report that you can download for free at the link below.

www.missingkids.com/adcouncil/pdf/lingo/onlinelingo.pdf

Computer Setup and Why Most Parents Get It Wrong

Some households have only one computer that is shared between family members and in some households everyone in the family has their own computer. Both scenarios will be discussed, in this chapter, along with general suggestions for setting up the computers.

Single Computer Households

If you have one computer shared by both parents and children, then it is critical that your computer is setup properly and everyone follows some important guidelines. If your children have complete freedom over the family computer, then it's very possible that their parents may become a victim of identity theft.

Current computer operating systems feature "user accounts" that allow various operations to be controlled by computer "Administrators". Every user on a shared computer should have their own user account that requires them to login with a unique password; this allows the permissions of each user to be controlled on the computer.

Windows XP and Vista Home Editions come with two basic types of accounts: "Administrator" or "Limited" accounts (or "Standard User" for Vista Home Edition).

Parents should be the only users with administrator accounts. Remember administrators have full control of the computer. Children should be setup with a limited account (or "Standard User" for Vista). The limited account restricts users from changing most computer settings and deleting important system files. Users with limited accounts cannot install software or hardware, but will still be able to access software that is already installed on the computer. Limited accounts can change their own password but can't change their account name or account type. Setting up your children with limited accounts will help prevent Spyware or any other program from being installed without your permission. When user accounts are correctly setup, only the Administrators install programs and change system settings.

If your computer never required a password to login, then you will need to setup user accounts on your computer. Change the default account so it requires a password and this should be the administrator account for the parent. Add a new "Limited" (or "Standard User" for Vista) accounts as required for children and other users.

Important - Always be sure there is at least one Administrator account or no one will be able to change your computer's settings.

Basic steps for adding accounts are provided below. Complete instructions can be found by visiting the main page at your operating system's website (i.e. www.microsfot.com) and typing "setting up user accounts" in the search box.

The tutorials below will assume you are using Windows XP because it is the most widely used operating system at the time of writing this book. If you are using another Windows based operating system this may work for you as well.

How to setup user accounts for your kids

1.   Click Start
2.   Choose Control Panel
3.   Double-click User Accounts
4.   Click Create a New Account
5.   Enter the name of the person you are creating the account for. (Usually your child's first name or nickname)
6.   Click the Next button.
7.   Choose Limited for the account type.
8.   Final step, click Create Account

How to change a user account

1.   Click Start
2.   Click Control Panel
3.   Double-click User Accounts
4.   Click Change an Account
5.   Click the one that is labeled Computer administrator
6.   Click Create a password
7.   Follow the password instructions prompted
8.   Click Create Password

After setting up individual user accounts for everyone that uses the family computer and most importantly setting up the administrator account for yourself, check to make sure that when clicking on each account that your are prompted for a password. You don't want children or their friends signing on without a password, especially not into the administrator account.

Multiple Computer Households

Many families today are fortunate enough to have a computer for every child in a household and one or more for the parents as well. This option, when affordable can be a little safer for parents because it is less likely your children will be installing Spyware on the parent's computer putting you at risk to identity theft. However, having multiple computers in your household can make it much more difficult to monitor your child's Internet activity, who they're chatting with, and any programs they've installed on their computer for downloading illegal music files, playing inappropriate games and other activities.

One alternative that many parents use is to have multiple computers so each child can do their homework but just one computer with Internet access in a family room where everyone has plain view of the computer monitor. This has helped many parents monitor their child's online activities while regulating how much time they're spending on the Internet.

If you are going to allow your children to have Internet access in their own bedroom, then you should set yourself up as the "Administrator" on their computer and setup your child as a "Limited User" as discussed earlier in this chapter. This will help ensure that your child is not installing software to illegally share and download music. Make sure they haven't already installed P2P software as discussed in Chapter 9. Taking these steps, your child will be aware that you may be monitoring their Internet activity which should help to discourage inappropriate behavior online.

Parents must also remember to secure their own computers with a password to protect any Administrators accounts and reduce the risk of spyware and viruses from being installed.

Additional security steps will be discussed in the antivirus and Internet security sections in this chapter.

Unsecured Wireless Internet

Wireless Internet also known as Wi-Fi allows you to access the Internet anywhere in your house and usually a short distance around your house without the need for running Ethernet cables all over your house.

The most dangerous part of an unsecured wireless Internet connection is that anybody with a wireless Internet capable computer that is within range of your wireless signal can connect to your Internet service. One scheme used by computer hackers is to drive around neighborhoods with their laptop in their car looking for unsecured wireless Internet connections better known as "hotspots". Once a hacker connects they can sniff your traffic from your Internet connection, which will essentially give them the capability to see any information you're sending across your Internet signal like online banking, credit card numbers, etc…

An unsecured wireless Internet connection also would allow someone to download and share illegal music files, software, and movies which put you at serious legal and financial risk as previously discussed over 17,000 people have been sued for downloading media illegally. Another danger is that a sexual predator near your house can share child pornography pictures across your Internet connection. Unfortunately, it will be your door the F.B.I is kicking down and you may be in legal trouble for something you never did.

Remember you are responsible for your Internet connection. If you are using wireless Internet connections in your home, make sure that it is secured properly.

How to check if you use wireless Internet and if it's secure or not

To check if your Internet connection is secured, use the following steps:

The tutorials below will assume you are using Windows XP because it is the most widely used operating system at the time of writing this book. If you are using another Windows based operating system this may work for you as well.

1.) Click the Windows start button

2.) Click the Control Panel button

3.)   Double click the Network Connections button

4.)   Make sure your Wireless Network Connection shows the secure lock in the upper right corner

Wireless Network
Connection

If you are still uncertain, consult the instruction manual for your
wireless router as the setup of each router is a little different. If you do not
have a manual, most manufacturers provide a downloadable version online.

If you are not using a wireless Internet connection then most likely
you are connected directly through either an Ethernet or USB cable. Direct
wired connections do not have the same security risks as wireless connections. However, if your home network is setup to share files and printers,
you must be sure to secure the wireless connection or directly connected
computers will also be at risk.

Some ISP's provide modems with wireless capabilities that may be
enabled whether you are using it or not. Never assume that your router is
secured! If you are not using the wireless features, the best thing to do is
disable the connection which should be described in the instruction manual.
Many routers feature an LED that indicates if the wireless feature is enabled.

Antivirus and Internet Security Software

Antivirus software is commonly known as a computer program designed to pin point, erase and overcome malicious computer viruses that have been unintentionally installed without the computer users consent. As discussed in this book, there are many more dangers on the Internet today than just computer viruses.

Many Antivirus software packages commonly available today are primarily intended to eliminate computer viruses only. Some offer defense mechanisms from other threats as well. The good news is that most major companies now offer Internet security software that provides much more protection against the many threats that computer users face today.

The most important point to remember about antivirus software is that it must be updated frequently to recognize current viruses and threats. Some leading experts estimate as many as 600 new computer viruses are released every month, which is why keeping your antivirus software updated is critical.

Internet Security Software

Internet security software is functionally different than Antivirus software and it's important to know the differences when selecting the best package to use. Internet security software is designed to defend computer users against a wide range of online computer threats, including viruses, worms, trojan horses, phishing attacks, rootkits, and spyware. In addition, most Internet security software platforms offer defense against unsecured wireless Internet, spam (junk email) reduction, and parental controls.

The parental controls feature offered in many Internet security packages can be a very helpful tool for parents trying to regulate their children's online activities. Parental controls offer additional features that usually are not provided with the operating system. Controls include website filtering by age (like teenager, adult), content filtering, time limits, specific URL blocking, and many more. Many modern filters are heuristic and results are learned and improved upon with use. If the parents are correctly setup as the only "Administrators", children cannot change the security settings.

It's best to visit an online shopping site that provides a side-by-side comparison of the features provided when shopping for the best package for your family. www.cnet.com is one website that lists many Internet security packages while comparing functionality.

Of course because Internet security software offers more features than Antivirus software you can expect to pay more for it as well. At the time of this printing, package deals were available costing around $20 more than Antivirus software and the difference should be well worth the investment.

It's important to note that even the best Internet security software cannot provide protection against all the dangers and threats that you and your family face online. Internet security software typically references a list of known viruses, spyware, and threats that are detected. This protects against known viruses and threats but just as computers and software are always advancing so are computer hackers and the threats they are spreading.

Remember the greatest threats and dangers come from criminals preying on the youth or any unsuspicious person. Do not install Internet security software and forget about the most serious threats of all from online predators, illegal file sharing, identity thieves, and the like.

Parents still need to play active roles in monitoring their children's Internet activity as suggested earlier in this book. Make sure you know the dangers discussed in every chapter of this book. The chapter outline in front of the book is a quick reference for any sections that may need to be reviewed. This book was designed to be easily understood and straight to the point so that even the busiest parents can breeze through it.

Cyberbullying

There was a time when the word bully would bring to mind the big bad kid that terrorized students by stealing all the defenseless little kid's lunch money. Today children are not only faced with bullies in school but online as well and in some cases it may be the same bully that's been tormenting them in school.

Tragically, some instances of cyberbullying have ended in teen suicide and that alone was reason enough to include this serious problem in this book.

One thing my parents always told me was that high school was just a small little part of my life and no matter how hard it seemed to be at times nothing was ever worth taking my own life. Although it seemed that high school, the peer pressure, and all of the problems associated with it would last forever, as I look back now the years flew by and truly were a very short part of my life. If your children are going through tough times, make sure to tell them the same thing my parents told me.

What is Cyberbullying?

Cyberbullying is basically when a bully uses the Internet to attack their victims through popular web technologies like social networking, email, blogs, YouTube, chat rooms, instant messaging, and text messaging. Cyberbullies often make hurtful remarks, threats, sexual accusations, and racial comments about their victims to break them down emotionally.

Undoubtedly, bullying has been going on in schools since the beginning of public education and there were frequent incidents during my years in school. Before cyberbullying, victims of this abuse could go home at the end of the day without dealing with the hurtful remarks and humiliation suffered in the classroom or hallways of school.

What makes cyberbullying so much more threatening is that the abuse never ends. The relentless attacks from the Internet continue without rest until they break down the targets of their aggression.

Cyberbullying Through Social Websites

Cyberbullies create fictitious MySpace profiles, create blogs, and use instant messaging, to intimidate their victims. If your child is the victim, the bully will post humiliating pictures, comments, and any hurtful garbage imaginable online about your child. Your child may then notice several other kids join in on the badgering. The misuse of social networking websites is so damaging and effective because once a spark is ignited the hatred spreads like a wild fire out of control.

An Action Plan to Fight Back

While laws of each state may differ, "Defamation of Character" laws have been adopted by most states and many jurisdictions are currently pushing to adopt cyberbully laws. In the United States it is a federal crime to anonymously "annoy, abuse, threaten, or harass any person" via the Internet or telecommunication system, without disclosing your true identity, punishable by a fine and/or up to two years imprisonment.

If your child is the target of cyberbully attacks, don't wait for the problem to escalate out of control; contact school officials or law enforcement immediately.

Here's a list of simple tips to follow if your child is cyberbullied through the use of a social networking website like MySpace.com:

1.   Don't respond to messages from the cyberbully.
2.   Delete the cyberbully from your friends list so they can no longer add comments to your profile.
3.   Block the cyberbully from contacting you anymore.
4.   Keep a copy of all messages the cyberbully sent to you as evidence in case you need it.
5.   Contact law enforcement or school officials for assistance and a course of action.

Cyberbullies often create a false profile that impersonates their targeted prey. They post pictures, send out messages and publicize any form of slander that will defame their victims. Depending on the type of abuse posted, this may be a form of identity theft and identity theft is a federal crime! Typically it's prosecuted as a Class C Felony, which can mean 2-8 years in jail and up to $10,000 in fines depending on the harm inflicted by assuming another person's identity.

Parents and victims of cyber aggression should be aware that the burden of proof rests on the victims in most cases. Be prepared to present emails, pictures, and other hard proof of your accusations before approaching authorities. Never respond or reply to emails or aggressive attacks as this would only aid your attackers by providing evidence to use against you.

If a cyberbully has created a malicious profile impersonating your child, contact MySpace or the social networking website that hosted the offensive content and they should promptly delete it for you.

YouTube Fight Videos

A new tactic used by cyberbullies is to intentionally pick a fight with a victim while an accomplice videotapes the whole fight. The bully typically starts a fight with a weaker individual that he undoubtedly would beat in a fight; they then would post the video of the degrading beating on You-Tube.com. Before you know it the whole entire school is watching the video, humiliating the victim even more.

If your child is involved in a similar fight, ask them if they noticed anyone with a video camera filming the fight and explain to your child your concerns and how the video may be used. Also be aware that many cell phones have video cameras built-in and some can record video for one or two minutes and even upload the video to YouTube.com.

If your child is the unfortunate target of this abuse, try to locate the video. There may be an option to mark (or flag) it as offensive. Next try contacting YouTube.com or the hosting site and explain the problem with the video. You can find a link for their contact information at the bottom of their website.

You should also consider whether or not this fight could be considered an assault. If you are able to find the video on YouTube or any other video sharing website the video could be used as evidence. Contact your local law enforcement or school administrators, if the event took place on school property to be advised on the best course of action to take.

One last important point to mention before closing this chapter, if your child is abused by a cyber bully they may not always tell their parents about it. If you notice changes in your child's behavior or if your child is depressed, ask them if they are having any problems or if they would like to talk about anything. Teenagers especially hold their emotions in and aren't always willingly to share problems with their parents.

With teen suicide as the third leading cause of death, the best policy is to be open and honest with your child. Stay involved in their life and always be aware of changes or warning signs that something may be wrong.

Wi-Fi Video Game Systems Give Kid's Unrestricted Internet

If you think the only way to access the Internet is by a computer, you may be in for a surprise. Many kid's have video game systems that allow access to the internet by Wi-Fi or direct connection through an Ethernet cable. Some hand held video game systems permit access to the Internet anywhere there is a wireless hotspot, which today is just about everywhere.

Many high tech video game systems are powerful enough to function both as a computer and video game system. In some cases they may require minor modifications to give it the capabilities of a home computer like browsing the Internet.

The ability to browse the Internet is not a feature that was available in video game consoles like the Xbox 360. Instead third party programmers have made modifications and provided the necessary software and instructions so anyone can make these modifications and many enthusiasts made the required changes to provide this feature.

Other video game consoles like the Sony PS3, Nintendo Wii, and the PSP (PlayStation Portable) make Internet browsing readily available and are constantly improving features to make it easier to use the Internet right through the game console.

The points to remember is that if your kid's have one of the latest video game consoles and you're trying to monitor their Internet access and restrict their computer activities, they may just be using their video game console instead.

Cell Phones

Most major cell phone service providers offer Internet features as an option on cell phone plans. This means that your kid's may have unrestricted Internet access to do just about what ever they want on their cell phones.

Using the Internet on cell phones may be slow and cumbersome but with advances in cell phone technology these features are improving. For example many cell phones now have full keyboards built into them to make text messaging and browsing the web much easier.

Check with your service provider to see if your kid's have Internet access on their cell phones. If so you're probably paying for it and these features may appear on your bill. Contact your service provider to see if there are any parental controls that can help you regulate and monitor your child's Internet activities.

If you decide that your kids do not require Internet access on their cell phones, cancel these features with your service provider. Be sure to inquire if these services can be activated remotely on the phone by using the features or you may end up with a bill for several hundred dollars.

As electronics devices increase in complexity and as features are enhanced, more devices will offer Internet connectivity. The best way to protect your children is to be involved in your child's life and remain aware of how they are using these technologies.

Drug Dealers, Pornography, Homemade Bombs, Oh My

Any of the dangers associated with life on the streets exist in some form or another in the electronic world of the Internet. Online drug dealers may be targeting your kid's or just as disturbing, your kid's may be able to find recipes online to make their own drugs from household items.

The Internet is a great tool when used properly but when used improperly it can be very dangerous, especially to children. In the absence of parental supervision, young curious minds are free to explore any activities or areas of interest, even those that would certainly not meet their parent's approval.

For instance some kid's have used the Internet to find make-it-yourself drug recipes, pornography, and homemade explosives or weapons. This kind of information and content should not be available to children online, but unfortunately it is and if you're not monitoring your child's Internet activity, it's possible that they may have access to it.

Online Drugs

If you find this too hard to believe, use any search engine to search for the word "robotrip"; you should see enough information to change the way you think kid's use the Internet. One search for "robotrip" returned a link to a video of a young kid that was experiencing a RoboTrip. There are also several forums of kid's talking about these experiences as well.

The Internet has been misused to become a resource for make-it-yourself drug recipes as well as new ways to experiment with household items and over the counter drugs. If you monitor your kid's Internet activity, you will know if they are searching for this deadly information.

Another danger is the phony drug pharmacies online that fill orders without a prescription, typically the most popular prescription drugs are pain killers.

Money is the force that drives these illegal drug dealers. If your kid has a debit card, you should be aware that most debit cards can be used as a MasterCard or Visa depending on the issuing bank, which means your child can make purchases online. Kid's as young as 14 years old have been issued debit cards, but typically someone that young must have their parents name must on the account as well.

If your child has a savings account and is interested in obtaining a debit card, talk to a bank representative at to find out if restrictions may be set to protect your child. If your child wants a debit card to make purchases online, you must monitor and know everything they are buying online.

Online Pornography

If you are like most parents, you don't want your kid's viewing any form of pornography online. Below are some statistics that have been provided by Family Safe Media.

- Every second - $3,075.64 is being spent on pornography
- Every second - 28,258 Internet users are viewing pornography
- Every second - 372 Internet users are typing adult search terms into search engines
- Every 39 minutes: a new pornographic video is being created in the United States

Children Internet Pornography Statistics	
Average age of first exposure to pornography	11 years old
Largest consumer of Internet pornography	35 - 49 age group
15-17 year olds having multiple hard-core exposures	80%
8 - 16 year olds having viewed porn online	90% (most while doing homework)
7 - 17 year olds that freely give out home address	29%
7 - 17 year olds that freely give out email address	14%
Children's character names linked to thousands of porn links	26 (Including Pokemon and Action Man)

Internet Pornography Statistics	
Pornographic websites	4.2 Million (12% of total websites)
Pornographic pages	420 Million
Daily pornographic search engine requests	68 Million (25% of total search engine requests)
Daily pornographic emails	2.5 Billion (8% of total emails)
Internet users who view porn	42.7%
Received unwanted exposure to sexual material	34%
Average daily pornographic emails/user	4.5 per Internet user
Monthly pornographic downloads (Peer-to-Peer)	1.5 Billion (35% of all downloads)
Daily Gnutella "child pornography" requests	116,000
Websites offering illegal child pornography	100,000
Sexual solicitations of youth made in chat rooms	89%
Youths who received sexual solicitation	1 in 7 (down from 2003 stat of 1 in 3)
Worldwide visitors to pornographic websites	72 Million visitors to pornography: Monthly
Internet pornography sales	$4.9 Billion

If you don't want your kid's viewing pornography, one way to help is to following advice listed in earlier chapters of this book to monitor your child's Internet activity. Do not allow your kid's to access the Internet using computers in their bedrooms or other remote places. Instead locate a computer for this purpose in a centralized place in your home where you can easily see what's on the computer screen at all times.

You should also routinely check the Internet history on computers your kid's use to browse the Internet, follow the advice listed in Chapter 6. Don't forget the Internet history can be easily erased, so the best option is to install parental computer monitoring software, similar to that mentioned in Chapter 6. This type of software will allow you to monitor your kid's computer activities even without their being aware of it.

Homemade Bombs

Another danger that attracts mostly young teenage males to the Internet is homemade explosive devices made with household chemicals. It may start out with some friends watching videos online of other kids detonating homemade explosives, until someone gets the foolish notion that they can do the same thing.

These videos often contain instructions and details on how to obtain the needed materials. The dangerous thing about homemade explosives is that most of them are uncontrolled chemical reactions concealed tightly in some sort of container. The uncontrolled chemical reaction exposes the container to extreme pressures causing it to burst often with unexpected results.

Many online videos show that these dangerous experiments often end up hurting someone. Due to their unpredictable nature, these devices may explode in the kid's hand or right next to him leaving the possibility of missing fingers, chemical burns, and dangerous flying shrapnel. In some experimental chemical bomb videos, the kid's come close to burning down their parent's home.

There are also reports of people who have posted videos or information online on making explosive devices which ends up with the FBI confiscating all the computers in the home and arresting the person who posted the information. Typically the types of explosive devices you see online that kids are making won't result in the FBI kicking down your door, but if your kid finds a deadly concoction and posts a video online, it is a possibility.

If you want to see the kind of chemical bombs kid's are making then posting videos for anyone to see, go to www.youtube.com and type in the following key phrases:

"Works Bomb"
"Chlorine Bomb"
"Chlorine Bomb Gone Wrong"
"Homemade Bomb Accident"
"Homemade Bomb Gone Wrong"

Watching just a few of these videos should be enough to convince any parent that homemade bombs and similar information are yet another cause of great concern for parents today with all types of information readily available on the Internet.

Going Forward

The Internet will always pose many new dangers to you and your kid's. In an attempt to help keep parents informed of any new dangers as they are discovered, an email update service will be made available to purchasers of this book.

Sending updates to my readers through my email newsletter will eliminate the need for a revised copy of this book to be purchased. As updates become available you will be notified through email. Publishing updates by email will also eliminate the need for you to reread a revised book every time changes are made.

Updates will be made available for FREE as long as it is cost effective. This may have to be on a first come first serve basis so sign up now by visiting my website below.

www.InternetSecurityForParents.com/freeupdates

(We value our customer's privacy and make it a policy to never rent, sell, or share your email address with anyone!

Resources

<u>Top Search Engines:</u>

Google – www.google.com
Yahoo – www.yahoo.com
MSN – www.msn.com
Ask – www.ask.com

<u>Top Social Networking Websites:</u>

MySpace - http://www.myspace.com

Facebook - http://www.facebook.com

Friendster - http://www.friendster.com

Orkut.com - http://www.orkut.com

AOL People Connection - http://peopleconnection.aol.com

Zorpia - http://www.zorpia.com

Hi5 - http://www.hi5.com

Tickle - http://web.tickle.com

EveryonesConnected - http://www.everyonesconnected.com

Backwash - http://social.backwash.com

Twitter - http://www.twitter.com

Yahoo! 360° - http://360.yahoo.com

Xanga - http://www.xanga.com

Bebo - http://www.bebo.com

There are well over one hundred popular social networking websites and the trend will continue to grow. Below is a list of the top 100 social networking websites as ranked by Alexa.

Top 100 Social Networking Sites (Ranked by Alexa.com)

1 http://360.yahoo.com
2 http://www.orkut.com
3 http://www.facebook.com
4 http://spaces.live.com
5 http://www.myspace.com
6 http://www.hi5.com
7 http://www.friendster.com
8 http://www.fotolog.com
9 http://www.livejournal.com
10 http://www.xanga.com

11 http://www.bebo.com

12 http://www.multiply.com

13 http://www.linkedin.com

14 http://www.stumbleupon.com

15 http://www.gaiaonline.com

16 http://www.last.fm

17 http://www.piczo.com

18 http://my.opera.com/community

19 http://www.buzznet.com

20 http://www.imvu.com

21 http://www.twitter.com

22 http://www.squidoo.com

23 http://www.mybloglog.com

24 http://www.wayn.com

25 http://www.slashdot.org

26 http://www.blackplanet.com

27 http://www.ning.com

28 http://www.myyearbook.com

29 http://www.meetup.com

30 http://www.classmates.com

31 http://www.unyk.com

32 http://www.vox.com

33 http://www.faceparty.com

34 http://www.yuwie.com

35 http://www.yelp.com

36 http://www.hubpages.com

37 http://www.secondlife.com

38 http://www.nexopia.com

39 http://www.mobango.com

40 http://www.43things.com

41 http://www.tribe.net

42 http://www.fanpop.com

43 http://www.reunion.com

44 http://www.greatestjournal.com

45 http://www.care2.com

46 http://www.migente.com

47 http://uk.tribe.net

48 http://community.adlandpro.com

49 http://www.broadcaster.com

50 http://www.ecademy.com

51 http://www.couchsurfing.com

52 http://www.downelink.com

53 http://www.mog.com

54 http://www.gazzag.com

55 http://www.ryze.com

56 http://www.gather.com

57 http://www.zaadz.com

58 http://www.librarything.com

59 http://www.xuqa.com

60 http://www.directmatches.com

61 http://www.profileheaven.com

62 http://www.dogster.com

63 http://www.eons.com

64 http://start.aimpages.com

65 http://www.passado.com

66 http://www.ruckus.com

67 http://www.travbuddy.com

68 http://www.student.com

69 http://www.sosyalan.com

70 http://www.graduates.com

71 http://www.tagworld.com

72 http://www.takingitglobal.org

73 http://www.blurty.com

74 http://www.bizpreneur.com

75 http://www.deadjournal.com

76 http://www.mygamma.com

77 http://www.trade-pals.com

78 http://www.musicforte.com

79 http://www.consumating.com

80 http://www.meetin.org

81 http://www.wallop.com

82 http://www.mugshot.org

83 http://www.dandelife.com

84 http://www.dodgeball.com

85 http://www.groovenet.ph

86 http://www.itsjustcoffee.com

87 http://www.oyaye.com

88 http://www.socialgrid.com

89 http://www.tripconnect.com

90 http://www.decayenne.com

91 http://www.listography.com

92 http://www.flingr.com

93 http://www.kontakan.com

94 http://www.katropa.com

95 http://www.intellectconnect.com

96 http://www.bizfriendz.com

97 http://www.sitespaces.net

98 http://www.refer-online.com

99 http://www.yapperz.com

100 http://www.babbello.com

Top Video Sharing Websites

YouTube - http://www.youtube.com

Google Video - http://video.google.com

MySpaceTV - http://vids.myspace.com

Metacafe - http://www.metacafe.com

vidiLife - http://www.vidilife.com

Mefeedia - http://www.mefeedia.com

Dailymotion - http://www.dailymotion.com

Jumpcut - http://www.jumpcut.com

Vimeo - http://www.vimeo.com

Flixya - http://www.flixya.com

Putfile - http://www.putfile.com

Top Instant Messaging Programs

AIM - http://www.aim.com

Yahoo! Messenger - http://messenger.yahoo.com

Windows Live Messenger - http://im.live.com/messenger/im/home

Computer Help and Support

Microsoft Help and Support - http://support.microsoft.com

Apple Support - http://www.apple.com/support

About the Author

Dan Ivancic is a professional Web developer and Internet marketing expert who spends 40 – 60 hours a week on the Internet, marketing and maintaining websites.

He is the founder and editor of InternetSecurityForParents.com, a website devoted to educating parents about the dangers facing parents and their families on the Internet.

Dan is a Microsoft Certified Professional as well as a Microsoft Certified Database Administrator. Dan has attended various Internet security conferences put on by other leading experts in the field including the F.B.I.